NUCLEAR ENERGY

Nicolas Brasch

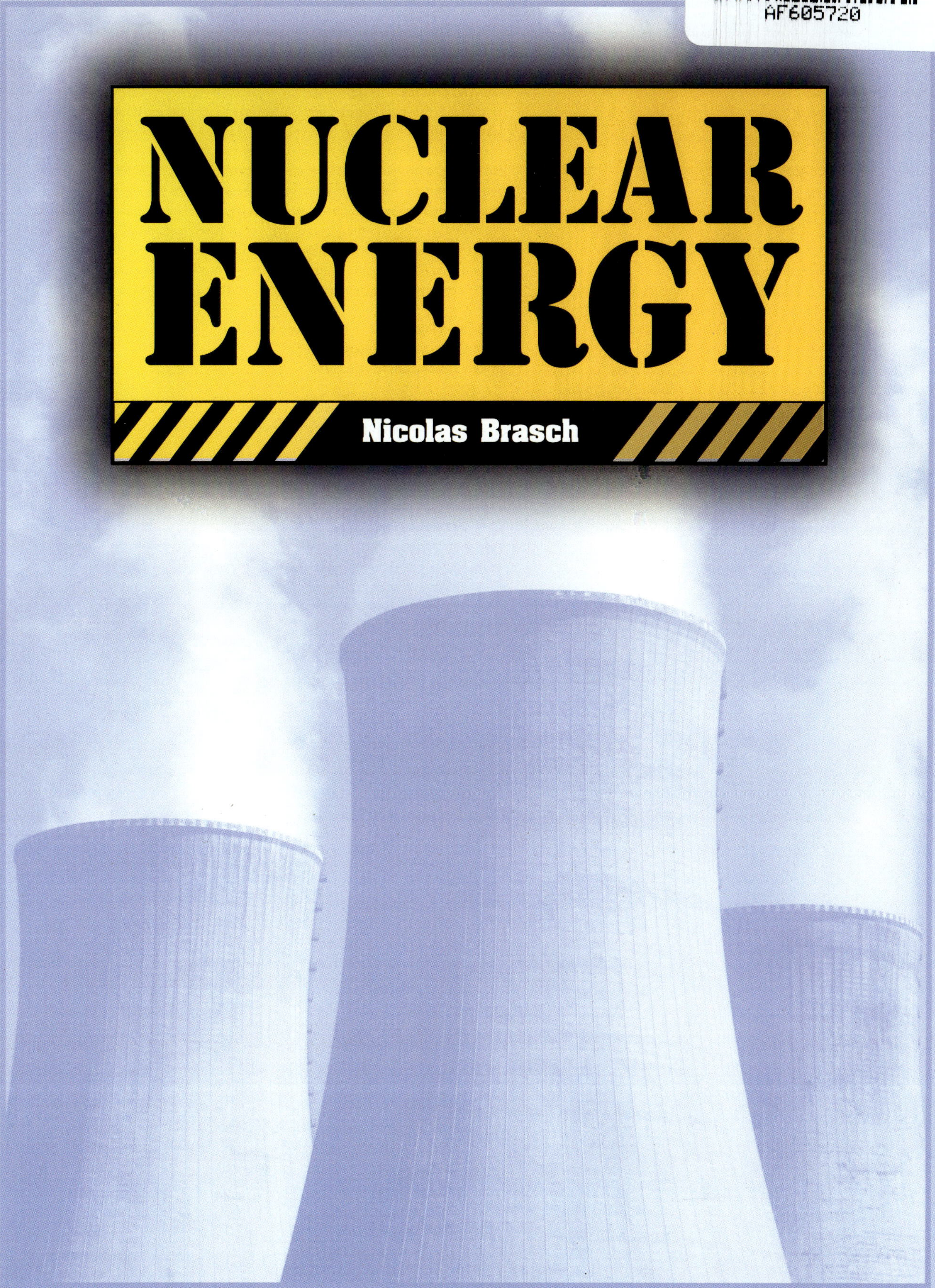

NELSON
A Cengage Company

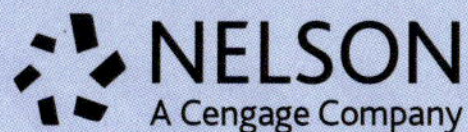

Australia • Brazil • Japan • Korea • Mexico • Singapore • Spain • United Kingdom • United States

Nuclear Energy

Text: Nicolas Brasch
Editor: Ben Haskin
Design: Jennifer Warwick
Series design: James Lowe
Photo researcher: Lisa Piemonte
Production controller: Adam Bextream
Reprint: Siew Han Ong

Acknowledgements
The author and publisher would like to acknowledge permission to reproduce material from the following sources:
Angelo Vlachoulis © Cengage Learning Australia: pp. 4, 6, 7, 11, 17; Corbis Australia: pp. 14, 16, 18, 19; Getty Images: pp. 20 (inset), 20 (main), 23; iStockphoto: p. 8; iStockphoto/Photovoltaik: p. 15 (inset); Newspix/Troy Bendeich: p. 10; Photolibrary: pp. 3, 5, 9, 12, 21, back cover; Picture Media/Reuters/Stringer Russia: p. 13; Shutterstock/Petr Nad: pp. 1, cover; Tamara Voninski/FairfaxPhotos.com: p. 22.

Every effort has been made to trace and acknowledge copyright. However, if any infringement has occurred, the publishers tender their apologies and invite the copyright holders to contact them.

Fast Forward Independent Texts
Level 25

For product information and technology assistance,
in Australia call 1300 790 853;
in New Zealand call 0508 635 766

For permission to use material from this text or product,
please email **aust.permissions@cengage.com**

ISBN 978 0 17 017952 2
ISBN 978 0 17 017899 0 (set)

Cengage Learning Australia
Level 7, 80 Dorcas Street
South Melbourne, Victoria Australia 3205

Cengage Learning New Zealand
Unit 4B Rosedale Office Park
331 Rosedale Road, Albany, North Shore NZ 0632

For learning solutions, visit **cengage.com.au**

Printed in China by 1010 Printing International Ltd
2 3 4 5 6 7 15

Contents

WHAT IS NUCLEAR ENERGY?

Nuclear energy is released from the centre, or nucleus, of an atom. Everything in the world is made up of atoms, including people.

Atoms are extremely small. They are so tiny that a million atoms placed one on top of the other could only be seen through a very powerful microscope.

Atoms are made up of protons, neutrons and electrons. The electrons move around the nucleus of the atom, which is made up of protons and neutrons.

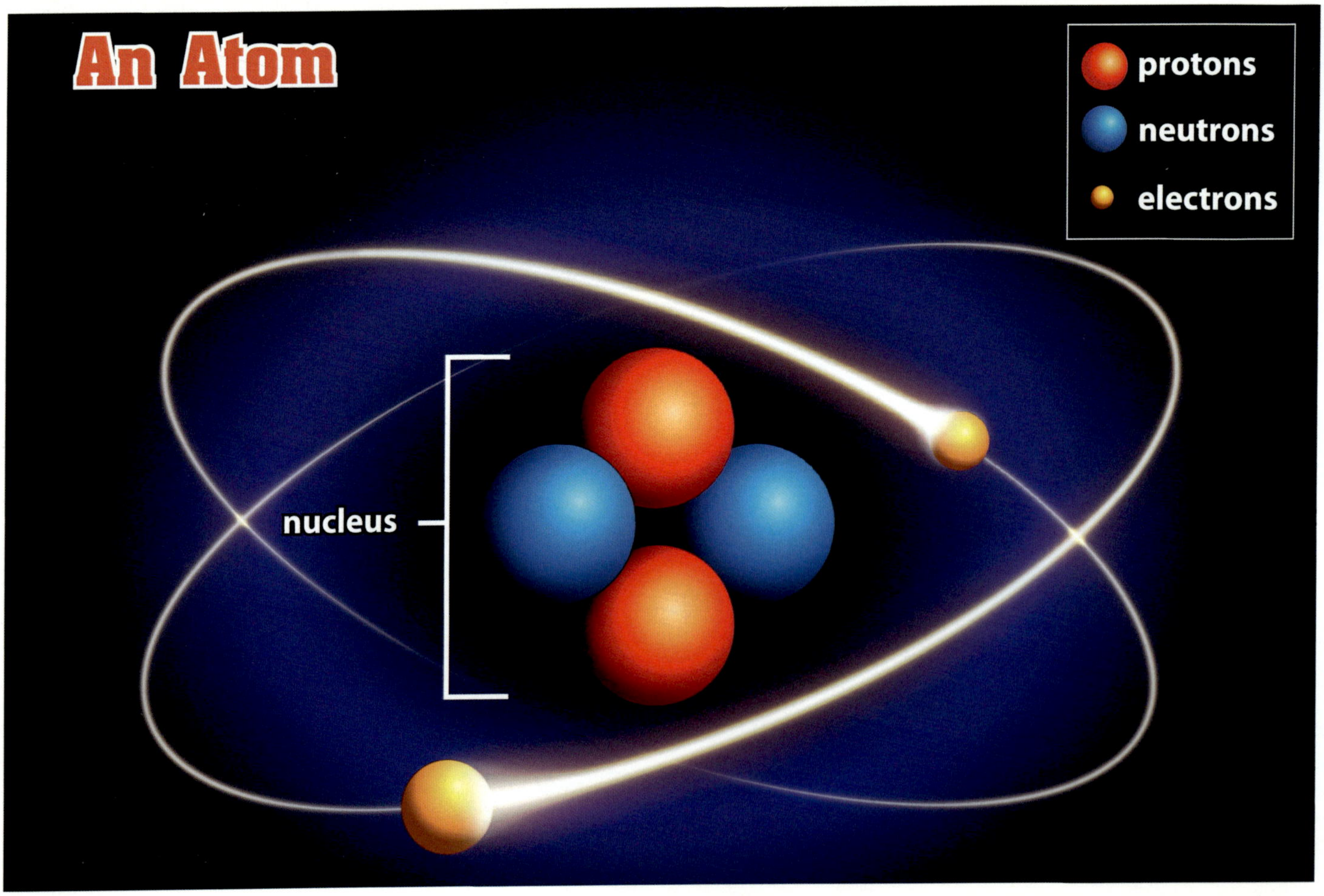

An Atom

protons
neutrons
electrons
nucleus

Scientists can only create nuclear energy from atoms with large **nuclei**, because they are able to break these nuclei. This process makes a lot of energy. The nucleus of a uranium atom is very large, so nuclear energy is usually made using uranium atoms.

Uranium atoms are found in minerals that are mined from the ground.

uranium being mined in Russia

CHAPTER 2

FISSION AND FUSION

Nuclear energy can be released in two ways: through nuclear fission and nuclear fusion.

Nuclear fission is the splitting of atoms. This is done by hitting the nucleus of a uranium atom with a neutron. This causes the uranium atom to split into two smaller atoms. When this happens, a large amount of energy is created, and some of the neutrons are released.

Nuclear power plants use fission to create energy.

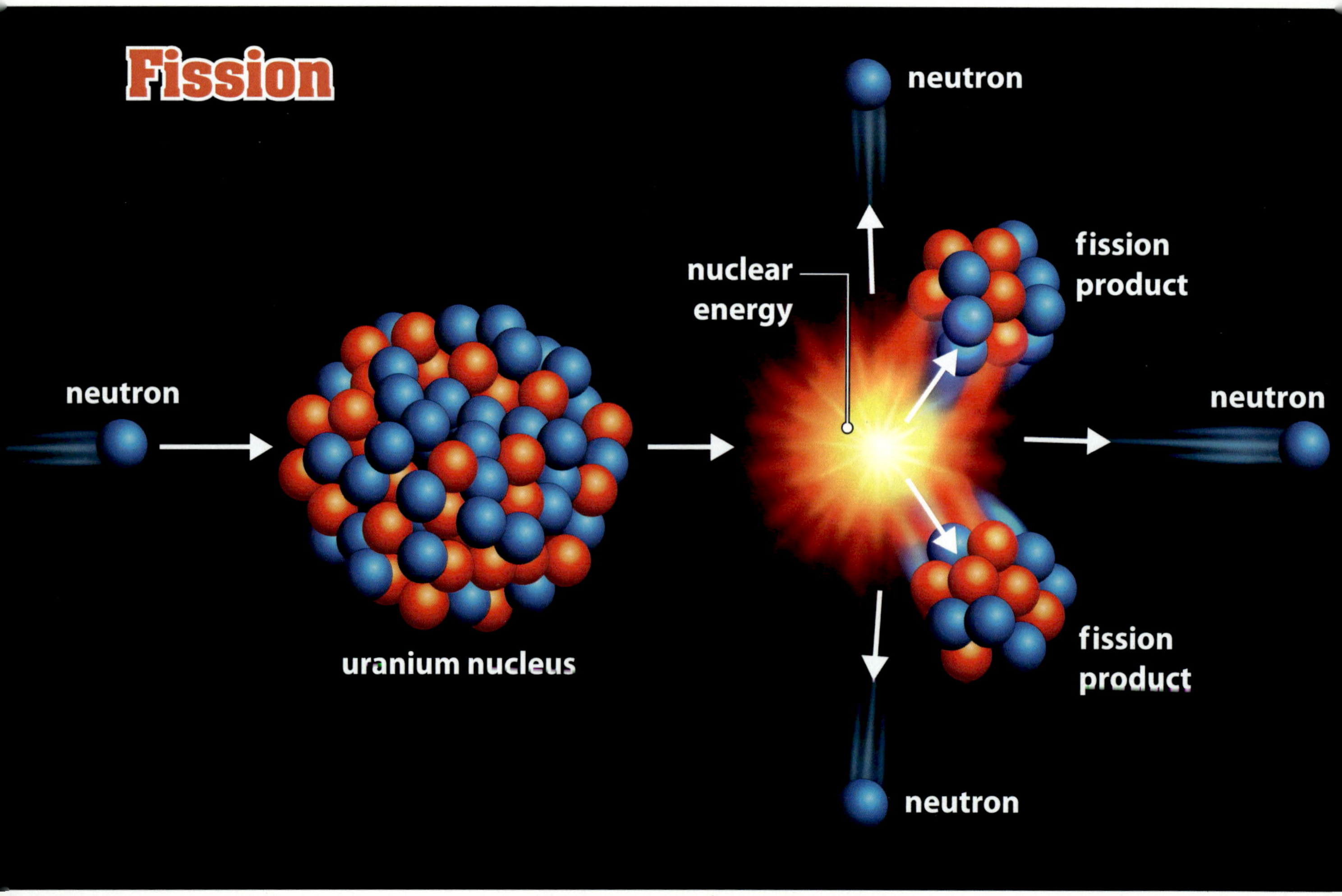

Fission

Nuclear fusion happens when two nuclei hit each other and form a single, bigger nucleus. This releases a lot of energy. The Sun's energy comes from nuclear fusion.

Scientists have found it difficult to create nuclear energy using fusion. It is hard to get the two nuclei to join together because they both have a positive **electric charge**. Unless the nuclei are forced very close to each other, they **repel** each other like two positively charged magnets.

Fusion

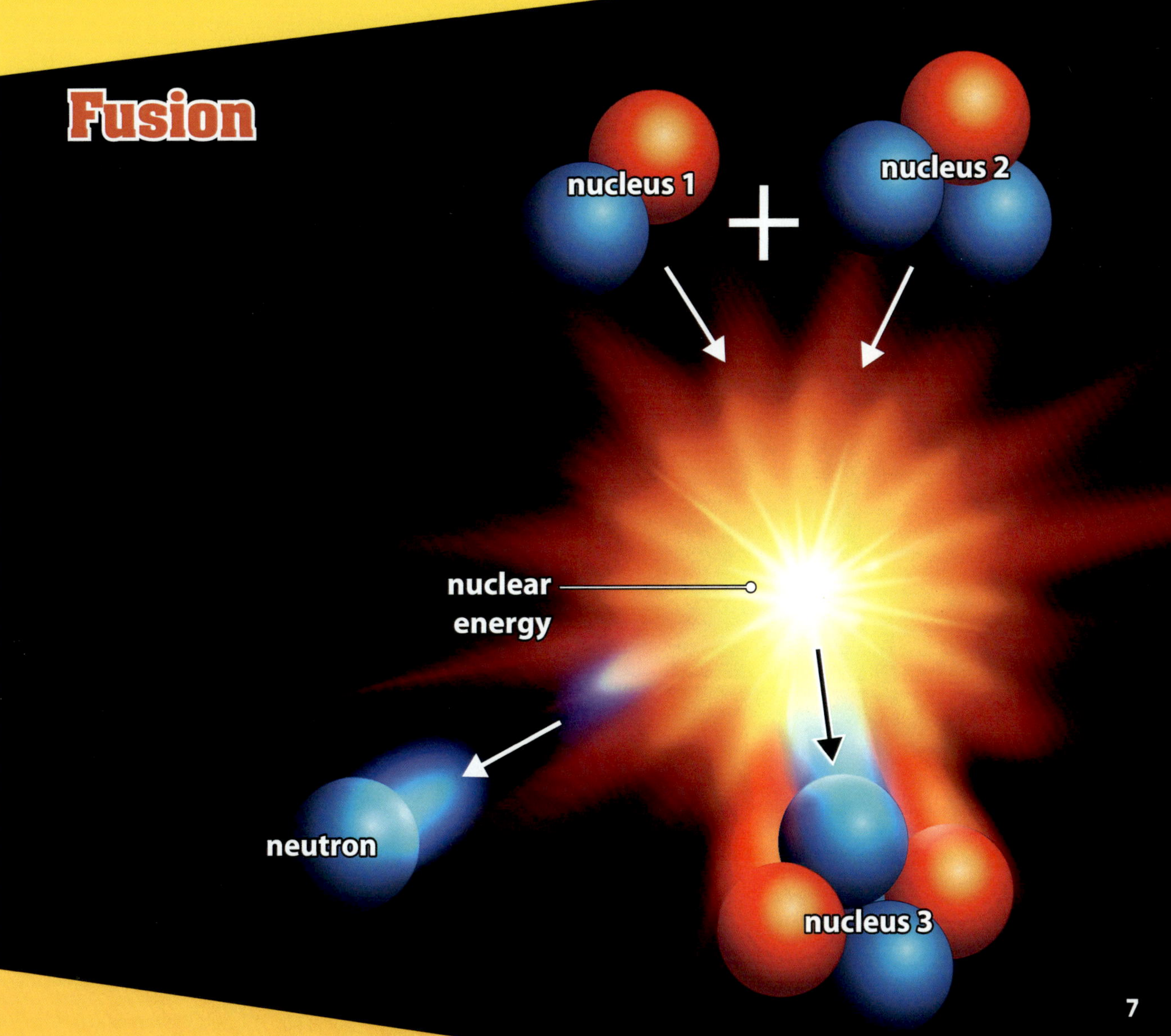

PROS OF NUCLEAR ENERGY

People in favour of nuclear energy give many reasons why it is a good source of energy.

They argue that nuclear power plants produce a lot less pollution than power plants that are run on coal or natural gas. A nuclear power plant produces around 12 times less greenhouse gas than a power plant that is run on natural gas, and around 30 times less greenhouse gas than a power plant that is run on coal.

a coal-fired power plant releasing air pollution

Nuclear power stations do not release as much greenhouse gas as other power stations because the fuel in ***nuclear reactors*** *is not burnt.*

People also say nuclear energy is better than energy made from fossil fuels because fossil fuels are **non-renewable** resources, and they will run out before long.

Fossil fuels are already in short supply because they have been the main sources of energy for people for many years. Nuclear energy is quite a new source of energy, and there is still a lot of uranium left in the ground.

Petrol is getting more expensive as oil supplies are used up.

Those in favour of nuclear energy also argue that nuclear energy is much more efficient than energy made from fossil fuels.

It takes only a small amount of uranium to produce a large amount of energy, so Earth's supply of uranium should last for a long time.

Earth's Uranium Resources

Finally, some people believe nuclear energy is good because nuclear power plants are usually safe places to work at.

If something goes wrong in a nuclear power plant, it can cause a disaster, so a lot of money is spent making them as safe as possible.

Technology is used to make nuclear power plants as safe as possible.

a rescued coalminer

On the other hand, coalmines are often very dangerous places to work at. There are many more accidents and deaths in coalmines than there are in nuclear power plants.

CONS OF NUCLEAR ENERGY

People against nuclear energy provide several reasons why it is not a good source of energy.

They argue that although there is a lot of uranium in the ground, uranium is a non-renewable resource like fossil fuels. This means that one day the uranium will run out altogether.

This mine was abandoned when it ran out of uranium.

They argue that even though nuclear power plants produce less greenhouse gas than power plants that burn fossil fuels, they still produce some greenhouse gas.

So instead of investing in nuclear energy, some people argue that it would be better to put money into improving renewable resources, such as wind and solar energy. Energy from the Sun and the wind will never run out.

Solar panels trap energy from the Sun.

Wind turbines create electricity from the movement of the wind.

Many people worry about the possibility of a nuclear accident. A major accident at a nuclear power plant could affect hundreds, thousands or even millions of people.

Some **by-products** of making nuclear energy are highly **radioactive**. Radioactive materials can cause cancer and kill people. A major radioactive leak at a nuclear power plant could kill people living within hundreds or thousands of kilometres of the plant.

Many people had to leave when an accident happened at the Three Mile Island Nuclear Generating Station in the USA.

On 26 April 1986, a nuclear reactor exploded at the Chernobyl Nuclear Power Plant, in the former USSR. This released a lot of radioactive **fallout** into the environment. The fallout was blown across Europe. This affected many people and polluted the land and water. The Chernobyl disaster is the worst nuclear accident in history.

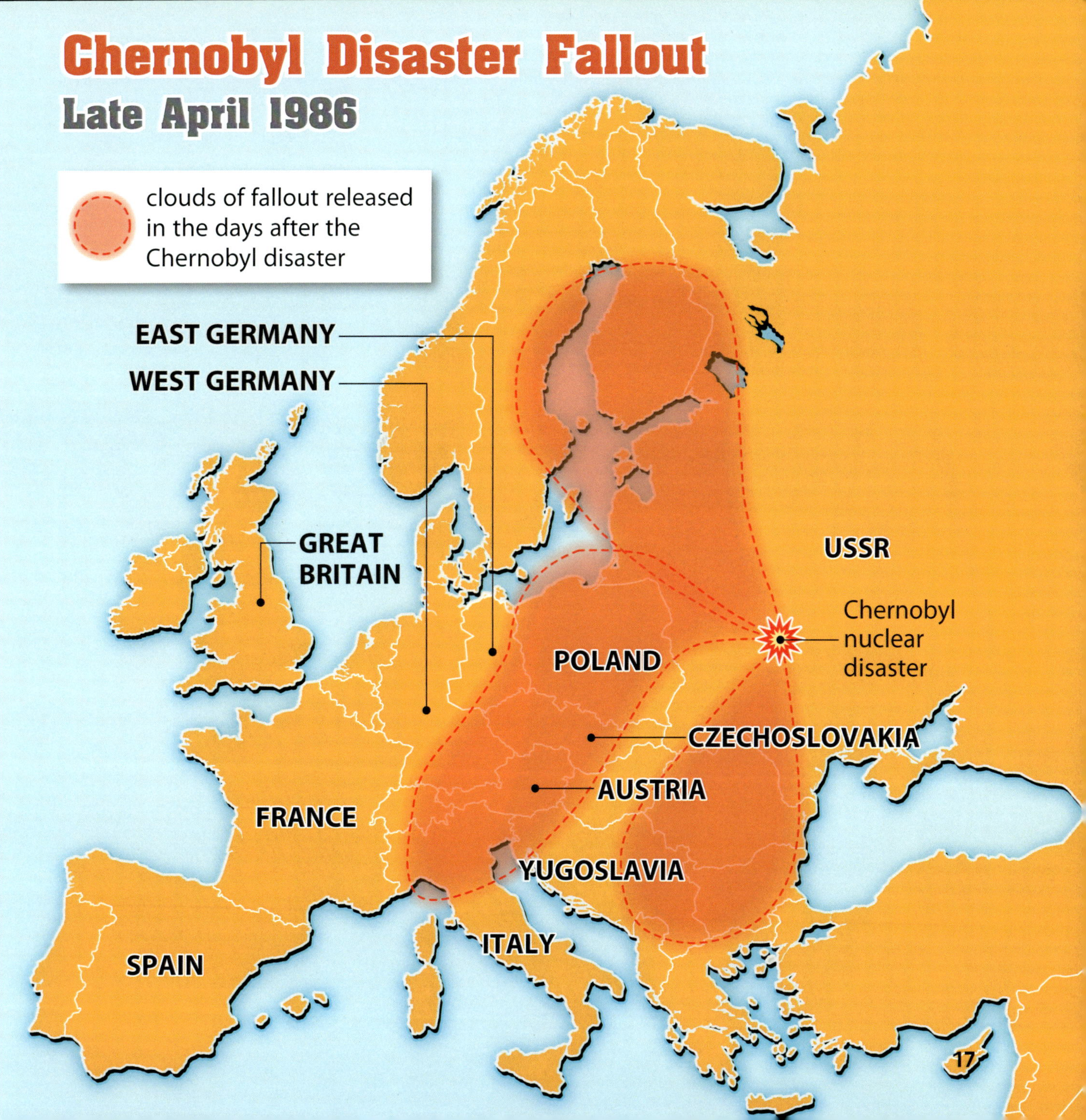

Another reason why some people do not like nuclear energy is because of the radioactive waste it creates. The waste stays radioactive for thousands of years, so it has to be stored underground where it cannot damage the environment in the future.

people protesting against the dumping of nuclear waste

storing nuclear waste underground

It costs a lot to store nuclear waste safely and it is hard to find suitable places to store it.

Another problem people have with nuclear energy is that its by-products can be used to make nuclear weapons. Nuclear weapons can cause more destruction than other weapons. They can even destroy whole cities.

a nuclear missile

The city of Hiroshima, Japan, was destroyed by a nuclear bomb in 1945.

There are international laws to stop people from making nuclear weapons. But some countries still use nuclear technology to make nuclear weapons. If this technology were not available, nuclear weapons could not be made.

testing a nuclear bomb

CONCLUSION

Pros

- ✓ Nuclear power plants create less pollution than power plants that are run on fossil fuels.
- ✓ There is a lot of uranium left in the ground.
- ✓ It only takes a small amount of uranium to produce a lot of energy.
- ✓ Nuclear power plants are usually safe places to work.

Australia has more uranium than any other country.

a protest against nuclear energy

Cons

- ✗ Nuclear energy comes from a resource that will run out one day.
- ✗ Nuclear energy produces some harmful greenhouse gases.
- ✗ A major accident at a nuclear power plant would be a disaster.
- ✗ It is hard to store nuclear waste safely.
- ✗ Nuclear weapons are made from the by-products of nuclear energy production.

Glossary

by-products	things that are created while making something else
electric charge	a basic property of very small particles, which can be positive, negative or neutral
fallout	a cloud of radioactive dust
non-renewable	not sustainable because of limited supply
nuclear reactors	devices where nuclear fission is carried out
nuclei	plural of "nucleus"
radioactive	giving off ionising radiation, a dangerous kind of energy that is released from nuclear reactions
repel	to push something away

Index